IN A LUTE

-THE CATHEDRAL

SILVIA EUGENIA CASTILLERO

Translated by

Victoria M. Contreras

MEDIO SIGLO

Las Lenguas de Babel Collection

MEXICAN POETRY IN TRANSLATION

First Printing 2018

ISBN 13: 978-0-9995119-1-6
ISBN 10: 0-9995119-1-2

Cover Design/Diseño de portada: Victoria Selene Cantú
Original Drawing/Dibujo Original: Victoria Selene Cantú

**This publication was made possible with the help of
the Translation Support Program (PROTRAD)
dependent of Mexican cultural institutions.**

**Esta publicación fue realizada con el estímulo del
Programa de Apoyo a la Traducción (PROTRAD)
dependiente de instituciones culturales mexicanas.**

www.librosmediosiglo.org
mediosigloeditorial@gmail.com

Harlingen, Texas
USA

PRINTED IN THE UNITED STATES OF AMERICA
IMPRESO EN ESTADOS UNIDOS DE AMÉRICA

IN A LUTE

-THE CATHEDRAL

SILVIA EUGENIA CASTILLERO

To José Ignacio,
José Eduardo,
and Ximena:
my three strongholds.

To José María –forever

To my parents, for their support.
And their everlasting companionship.

Portico

The Angel

He does not want to see the sky

he slides down the cord into

a sepia color gloom

in the opening of the columns.

He does not want the heaven, in his hands

the tremor:

rubrics of the land.

And his fingers lengthen the touch

over the nakedness of the vault.

Open wings;

but his body inclines

eager for the cold north wind and goats,

he goes with our step:

that angel.

To a Virgin

Pearly skin on wood in the center
of the altar, the virgin mocks history,
between grapes and veils smiles
voluptuously, the nymph, graceful
nubile, carries in her hands
the traces of love, in her glance
despises the norms, abandons
the innocent nakedness
of the angels. Prefers to hide behind
trees, foreshadowing a river
and fleeing, in wide-flowing escape
of forests and flashes. On the altar
the only star is the trace of her step,
a fanning smile
balances her charm.

Saint James

From the height

the saint with the translucent look

provides light

to the temple. Monolith poured into

incense towards the cardinal points,

he captures the rays of the sun. His eyes

seem to have glitter of quartz and agate

with seven red trees

inside and in its trunk

a hint of opaque speckled

skin. A glance of reddish

color, that are almost artificial circles.

From the back you reach the saint,

his eyes in perfection

become like a pure vault.

The Night

In the column Dionysus

proclaims as Triton the new

disorder, with mathematical skill

he organizes a meticulous night

but floods it with a mist, at an angle

without order he advances his law: now he joins

and favors, now discourages the muses.

His vine trees overflow

clusters on multitudes, they are arriving

from the east and south. The stone

bears the signature of the god in the form

of grapes and clandestine roses.

The abrupt rock

rises in a stormy way.

Devils

Those dusts

of the universe remain between

the shoulders and the gestures:

in the prudence of the stone.

After surviving for so long in its cut form

these are stealthy versions,

lives falsely woven,

in a whirlwind they burn the eyes

of bas-reliefs and

adjectivally break

the expression of the statues.

Those devils dissolved

in the dust of the centuries.

Earthly Devils

The earthly devils

like to walk alone

-in the interval-

like the cracks with their beak

to separate the end

from the beginnings. It was

a devil boy, in the pure

happening and he knew how to lull

death: to remain

with his round mouth,

eating bread, with his tongue

still red, with his heart

gray now, now stone.

Fiery Devils

The fiery devils

look like illegitimate stars:

Some slit the throat of smiling figures,

others laugh at universal grief.

To flee from the stone

they take over the red,

they take as their own the most absurd

inflections of the faces,

until arriving at the edge where

some immortal gesture

that returns them to the world

awaits them.

Colorless Devils

The beginning of darkness discerns

a change of light,

they are the colorless devils

dividing lines

between the abyss and the continuous.

In the dawn, they do not want

the boundary, they contaminate the

daybreak with a no-beginning. Fugitives,

without body,

they lull to sleep the ardent

and announce trembling

in light lines

a kingdom in flight.

Air Devils

The air devils are indiscreet,

because of them God made the world

wake up sane one day.

They were seen balancing between avid

smiles, hopeful eyes,

open mouths, calm postures:

they sculpted the hidden life of men.

The sculptures were growing in the vaults,

the belief in life

increased, the devils'

worshipers wandered to

the basement of the world. And God

set order in the cosmos.

Silhouette

The brown plaster

rooster, evades its unsteady

outline of feathers. On branches

without stems its feet await,

they stop a possible scene:

now they lose sharpness, now they are

definitive lines; then

from the imprecise line, the struggle

between its silhouette and the wall rises.

A Window

In the outline of the acanthus

and in angle with the night,

an incomplete window

useless between the stone,

cackles, paraphrasing absences,

its emptiness could

welcome us, but its form

still recalls,

its being does not end,

with its blurry lines , it balances itself.

Reflections

Concealed

that line blends

the liturgy of the stone,

its rippling of water comes

carrying the rubble of the road,

a spiral and then another

thrown into the void like a bridge.

A light and metallic stroke,

ponders senselessly an advance

of light.

Mirage

We follow the river,

a path

of uncertain formation

showed the double aspect of its shore:

the ambiguous light

illuminated

thick branches and stones,

it was the progression of the water

dry for later,

running water but scarce

at the point of being lost

inside the earth,

devoured by thirst.

The route was not a riverbed:

it was the silhouette

in one afternoon's desire.

The Earth Is Thickened

From the leaves

a stone slows down

as in a walked path;

it is the poplar, the chiseled column.

From the poplar a tunnel,

the most dense, thick,

tamped down, delayed earth,

burns perhaps from some proper name,

it rides.

Oratory

They are scratches, there among the rock

at the top of the mountain;

pleas attached to the stone

babble. Is your face

turned a parallel of voices,

your eyes delayed in the effort

of a monolith dotted with signs.

You still make yourself visible:

fold after fold you bury your flame with its reverse

into someone.

Arch

Abrupt and as without anyone, that arch

is held back behind the prayers. Chapel

waiting for the wandering. In that deserted area

of the crossroads, the arch challenges firmly

the rain that falls and crumbles it into golden

[particles

it thus becomes a frieze suspended beyond the river,

rusty in its own reflections like a sword.

Stained Glasses

Sketch

The folds barely sink in oil
and the whitish lead of the virgin
body dawns;
within a range of canvases
-in the diurnal blue of the silk-
the indigo becomes cautious
and relates the exceptional case
of the sunny red that crossed the fabric.
Intense, of cochineal and lacquer,
it is bleeding blue and it comes from alchemy:
the virgin is a sketch,
fiction of sulfate and potash.
Made of impurities,
with its silky cyanide skirt it is harmless,
it keeps its cosmetic formula
secretly as a sacred history.

Lasting Miracle

In the steep mantle, a river,

the silk marks are glazing of red lacquer,

there the shadows stop:

a gesture and eyelids. That cobalt

woman hiding in the whites

is intermediate, medium between resolved blacks

and the reds of failure. She does not look, she just

rocks cautiously above the rocks. She searches

in her body a verdigris meadow. But her mantle

is stony, rough as terracotta.

In her aspiration she seeks the overseas: she wants

to bathe in a river of incense with spices.

Exotic queen of sumptuous hues: she dreams.

Black Virgin

In the stone the virgin like, purple face

emerges;

it is a prickly, imperfect lily.

And it collapses into yellow roots,

struggling with shadows: blackness prevents

its celestial ascent - magnificent.

A realgar of strange orange

and copper pigments

becomes multiple in its desire:

bursts of bronze and gestures of gold.

That dry orphaned face

-polished in arsenic and mercury-

lives bound:

fossil of a virgin sealed and contained.

Vault

I do not understand that face,

crystal, pure light,

is it an unraveled gaze?

Border touching

the mist of looking at each other

Does it have a course?

It's a shiver creeping up my furtive,

unusual body,

contour sharpened with dates.

It strangles – it colonizes me–

it gets extinguished in me.

It is an isolated perfection:

a trembling of vowels,

an announcement of air

- a wall.

Width of time.

I do not understand that face,

acrobatics in the eyes

to go up to the vault.

And the reflections stutter.

An incomprehensible face

burns against the sky.

Saint Michael the Archangel

And the night: a dome becomes a vessel.

Beyond the columns and statues,

beyond the stone and its blinded eyes,

the gold born of the dying dragon distills

brightness like an electric shock.

A sky full of fangs and fissures,

returns an iris to the night

and the dome opens.

What was the dome but glow,

the claws of the monster

banishing the saint that kills it,

he sinks a staff in the jaws

without knowing that from them he has extracted

                              [the solar fire.

Not the retracted light but the flame.

Candles

Ashes,

confusion of air and water

from the silver color reflection

to the horizontal black.

And come back again and again

sharp, insistent its mystery:

from the celestial haze

to the sacred humidity. The line

of the slight, incorrect, absurd

forms, blurred in pure blue,

in the obsession of being only a hue,

and entangle the memory in its own resistant

residues like quartz but shooting,

baking crystals.

And the vapor in the leap of light

rusts, pulverizes, corrodes.

The Monk

Settled lines – like rain –

near the edges of the mantle

bring a light of rivers,

the drops must have been sparkling

gold dust caught in its brightness.

Settled lines, lament tuned

in a corner of a church,

they surround the cloak -big leaks-

dripping gold, pale,

weathering yellow,

the same melody as the last rain,

extended leather sprouting

from the yellow. And the monk

with closed mouth is wrapped

between pentagram lines,

Does he sing of his death?

Spike grains come from the yellow,

the parapet of the well absorbed

in the sheave, up and down,

split moments in multiple gold,

rampant yellow rounds in circles

until touching the edge of the ceiling

-the monk's lips, perhaps-

multiple corners form

the threshold star.

The road begins

in the mordant gold,

over the irregular mist of light

where the brown dominates

and gold forms between shadows

its kingdom of opacity and stone:

the shimmering glow begins,

tunic of the saint

where the golden and saffron are forged.

The light blossoms – over the land.

Shadows

Resin grains,

then the copper in salts

form the edges of the picture;

verdigris first, festive,

brown after-the green has disappeared.

It leaves the foreground and goes back

where nature

changes, doubts, blackens.

It faces time and it is poisoned,

from the lead it drinks the forces to be able to be
                                        [folded

and folded and creased, to be a marker.

Without evil the light wants to be prominent,

to become truly a form, with its setbacks;

to show the back of things,

the stains of life:

its drama.

Allied with time light is temporary,

it betrays its brightness, slips in its appearance

and fades. Shady and cloudy,

the rough lighting

weakens itself.

High Altar

The agony of yellow looks down on

the clusters of the altar,

vanished like sour fruit,

but the light insists on being correct

and now illuminates incandescent

-fictitious- Milky Way blues,

now the brown violet of remote

sand dunes.

Like wine in the mouth,

in the tongues of the faithful

is vividly corrupted , god in its contrast

-carmine and cobalt-

breaks colorless.

Prayers

Prayers saturate the air:

like leeches they invade

and undermine the fragile image of the saint.

In the corner, he remains

with his tired body

and extreme silence on his face:

for years the darkness covered him

and without further ado -doors inside- he finished

aging among the monotonous rhythm of prayers.

There are no more muscles that torment him

nor a troubling breath.

The saint strayed from time.

His proud heart became indifferent

from the colorless shore.

Tunic

In the monk's tunic

there are residues of keratin,

a kind of cornea that looks,

like coming from the vermilion.

This viscous robe, of living mobility,

has fibrous, abrupt, keloid lines.

There is an observant on the fabric,

his almost metallic being annoys

with so much crystal light.

Under the monk's robe

a swarm of silhouettes.

Cutaneous red,

goes over the caustic wrinkles

of a masked skin.

Mask

Tribute to Kôbô Abe

He shows a false happiness and borders

his lips with pigments.

The dividing line on the skin

is a mask;

then the vacuum is perceived inside.

Tubes connected

centimeter to centimeter,

rigid from the chin to the hair.

The eyes in the wrong direction,

at a sharp angle and fighting with the space.

A face without sunlight

where thorns sprout and swell

to become resentful sea urchins.

The forest without the north wind devoid of a
                                    [clearing

spreads its sultry mist

- whitening bandage-

forgetting to touch its temples:

the sensation is something more than merely the void

because there are no stripes of light or pores;

there are no glands nor veins,

the shadows are violet monsters:

skin without wrinkles devoid of sweat.

Under the Light

In Tyre, a Phoenician city, a dark princess

appeases the fury of the gods.

In the exodus from white to yellow,

from green puberty to eroticized blue,

she discovers within herself a drop

of purple tones, tincture or brilliantine,

drop that falls flat to the heart:

she offers the imperial indigo coming from the earth

and ignites the flirting of the gods

when under the bright light

she is reflected and in the vibration of the divine eye

disappears mysteriously.

The Raven

I have a crow-lead

attached to the foot

with its weight and nostalgia.

It looks at me with a strange face,

in mercurial tones it pretends to look.

It smells – it approaches- like a liquid sulfur

that has settled, prismatic;

it assumes its false colors.

Black, that crow like a stone,

without leaps it is still tied to my ankle.

It has been there for a long time, all night,

the night and the pillars of the temple.

That raven rises, shines,

repeats pink series;

it is born and is always extinguished at my feet

like vibrant sand.

Tumor and fissure,

the crow reverberates

-gold or light.-

The Last White Deer

Through the peephole passes a white deer

trapped in its gallop.

They are four corners

and a sun.

Because the deer takes the dawn,

the antlers grow towards

the unlimited white.

The peephole perhaps lies:

a torrential tap of reflections

multiplies the close to star

whiteness.

Something unearthly goes up:

a comet. Flying horns

in search of a body.

There is no body, no dawn, nor stars.

An empty room: only tiles

with deer in the center carved in stone.

Church

Rough texture:

Infidels and believers mix.

Pure light.

And the imprecision of contours

falls in the intimate layers,

to join spaces with surfaces.

The agonizing glow also

keeps us there.

Gradations and glazes

attach to the pious image,

but the construction reconciles

orange spots with green grass

and the white of the saints' countenance

disappears: a seizing of the pure

blends sensations with pigments.

Colors are formed.

Olive

The black olive mediates

between intense greens and

the muted tones of the earth.

It mediates between the gaps

and the trembling leaves. It looks like

a foolish beige that does not give in

to the fleeting of yellow, the black olive

is intermediate, the pause

from brown to scarlet; without austere

branches adjusting warmth

the olive tree would be a dam for the light.

Of pure opaque earth,

a forgotten jute in the middle of the plain.

Arbitrary, red and green, it is acid,

turbulent becomes red blood,

screams and in the wild becomes sacred.

Gobelin

On the verge of sinking into the night

the blue abandons its gloomy shade,

it enters that darkness of diaphragm

(melancholy as a way of life)

without intensity: only an intermediate being

between light and vacuum.

The confusion of a stony threshold,

suspended between the golden and vermilion,

between the pure and the terrible;

macerated in contrast

with iron. Grilled, waste

of divine dust, the blue deposits

in its pigments parts of the sky,

the foreign drops and a pinch of river.

Clay, flaxseed, bleach,

dry blues that will be quarry or leather,

perhaps a lacerating tapestry.

Underground Lake

Water inflames the stone,

an inner arch of light

forms waves between pillars.

The circular base

describes the stay of half reliefs:

imprecise nymphs, sirens?

The medusa turned into

gold and magnesium;

a female who is not a virgin

in red without a crown,

bathing like a moon

in the hollow of the oak.

The well that is abbey

- underground lake –

resolves its reflexes

in a clear beam of light

and rises in pointed arches.

Main Vessel

The Space

The vase is witness

of its iron syllables.

Without lips. Without hesitation.

Without a city on the river

Marguerite dies.

It is the water without drops,

the silent water of prisoner Marguerite

muttering. And the outrageous space

inhospitable undermines one and the other. Any

[angle.

Two and three: a cavity. Without hearing.

Without trembling. On her lips closed wind.

Obstinacy of the prison

to possess her.

In the city of the river

Marguerite lives stunned,

possessed of silence. She lives within herself.

There They Burn

Black tunics. Red hot cloaks. Skirts, sandals. Fabrics. There they burn. On her back. She is the daughter of Zion, fearless. Fugitive of love and its abandonment. She came to burn in this fire of guilt. She comes back from the dock. She was a column and a scepter. She was a meadow of gazelles. Purple Towers. Scarlet ribbons. Sentinel. She came to burn. Countless voices go through her. But she is quiet. Only scraps of rumor neaten - flatter. The lady falls among piles of cloth. A courtesan? The mouth full of dirt.

The Oblique Lady

Genevieve, Marguerite,

the oblique lady.

From the nodal depths, searches, gestating

the madness of faith without lights, without
                                                    [grammars.

Oblique, she burns her blood at the stake,

her hairs stand on end with the fire. In the gloom

the reds seem to extinguish. The golden colors

of her decoration possess the body

made strand, phosphorescent ribbons, parts

which fall stiff to the ground and become medallions,

bronzes, shields defending her

from the bustle of the fire that consumes her

and from the rumors of the crowd in front of her.

Oblique, she resists failure. She laughs, her discovery

of God is charred , there is no God, he does not come,
                                        [nor does he elevate her.

Her glimmer in contrast,

lasts through the night.

The Trap

What an appearance-that of the angels-they take the smell from bread without liking it. They do not feel. They do not see whiteness. What an appearance – that of the angels – they tread on the manure, they want to go unnoticed in drought. Without transparent light. And the branches rot, they put out the candles. They subtly corner themselves-praying. What an appearance - that of the angels - without shouting they are savage, they hurt the iris of the nubile attempts, without despair they intoxicate, they intensify, they aim with their violent waiting, they abuse their being half-way.

-Listen-, Christ bleeds.

They do not see him.

They subject us to the trap.

Dazzled

In front of the light -incandescent-reflectors, cameras.
The parade, the fashion, the bastings of the dress.
Phoenix you raise, stumbling among the veils, old rags
of antiquity on the skin. Unbelieving or turbid, you
ride your steps, walkway, edge, you want the rough
without the subtle. That unscathed walk quiets the
wound of the burning belly, hell tormenting you to
judgment. Mountain, plain, a full valley to keep
oblivion like a fruit falling from the fire. Sections of fire,
of light in small crestfallen fireflies into nothingness
together in incense. You confuse a thousandth part
with the whole, astonished you go, dazzled by
costume jewelry and phosphorescent fabrics. Without
soul. You do not scream, you do not plead: you model
beauty but you fall. You do not beg. You are waiting
for wealth. All present and future creatures that you
have been pass through the spectrum of your burning
figure. From profile and front you are a thousand
people, a body and a heart: you strongly defend the
lightness of your color and your form: every time

older, grown, total. That's why I curse you. And you continue on the red carpet.

Far Near

No longer of love nor of hate.

A spill of color in the eyes

of those who walk by.

Without listening to each other. A spill of vowels

when people laugh.

Between screams like those of bewildered flying
                                        [birds,

you can see lightning in the middle of a boulevard, a

patio with clothes lines crossing.

Without clothes hanging. That far near is an opening

in the middle of the sidewalk. And I passed in a hurry
                                        [and stumbled

And not even God stayed with me. The sky opened

but it immediately closed its clear movement.

Its porous surface of peace or rest:

far near. The soul saw a long movement

which disappeared at the same instant of being.

In the middle of the street.

Meanwhile

While you prepare the mouth in filigree and teeth tremble without being seen, as you become a nobody (*the will that produced the desire is dead*). As you put on lipstick behind the wall and advance lightly as when you went to the pool at midnight and crossed the reflection of the stars. While you are looking for an argument in your head and half open your lips, that nothing grows and fills all your sensation (*the will that produced the desire is dead*). While the dawn dew splashes your gaze, your footsteps travel through that avenue where the train stops and the coming and going of your memory go to your heart. From there you come, with the coffee cup still touching the corners of your mouth and the smell on your fingers. You cross the threshold, you undress, you look at yourself without mirrors, you feel the prayers of others (*the will that produced the desire is dead*). You know everything, you have everything, you want everything. And your ashes end in nothing.

Riverbed

The lights went out. It appeared with shores-crude- an echo. Pilgrim sound, a feline- you would say. An open riverbed to offer you the sea. I have no reason – it says. I hear it complete, without words, it takes it like a gaze through the open riverbed. Echo and fluid - current - is the misunderstood voice that passes. Without thirst. Without knowing. It unites truth and rudeness. It schemes a bit of wonder with the edges of the water. Down the riverbed, turned into the nothingness of the day, it disappears.

Wings

Stingers in the afternoon. An abrupt

change of the sun on the countenance.

On the greens the skin,

a crust of the sun comes out.

Her torso changes.

Only skin and a dream. Thus is born

the overture that hurriedly

opens as lightning:

it is desire. A stain.

Fearful the instant closes.

Only wings:

on the eyes three pairs. Birds

of the air and beasts that shed the skin.

They lurk, devour.

Wings closed under the face of the lady

-open.

The High Cedar

The high cedar falls off into broken branches, branches fading between sap, burning branches, splintered and hollow wood, empties its marrow by the fire. Incisor. The high cedar has among its branches an eagle, or perhaps an eagle's nest, the memory of the eagle and its nest, the highest flight of the eagle. Not the eagle. It possesses in the clarity of its brilliance, of its fire, in its own heart that burns in hundreds of splinters, the rays of the sun, the radiance of the sun, the tribulations of memory. The eagle matures - in flight - joyful in its dissolution. Between wanting and desire it burns, it burns in the high cedar, it burns enraptured. In the high cedar, in the abyss - among memories - like the flight of an eagle. Like a nest. It burns.

The Distance

Chronicles, minutes.

Minutes, feathers - the silence.

Plumage, birds, tones and reverberation.

The lady returns. It is the climbing

fire: it burns, it corrodes, it cancels.

And something is growing.

Clear surface

-faraway-

the soul is emptied,

it becomes surface: it reflects,

it begets. The divinity is

certainly remoteness,

the countless distance.

The God who never came.

The illusion of recognizing him,

the journey and from there

again the distance.

But the eyes may dare

not to be,

to grow towards where its form never did.

There where the gaze balances

its ignorance, the daring eyes

look back,

which is the same as seeing inside.

SONGS

On the Eve

Bells, wounds, lights--her belly dead. Men, prayers, threats, faults, joys - her body bare. The light is destroyed. Rolling among the edges of a foreign language, *inclinativ, inclinativ ex hoc in hoc* -she puts her memories together. He departs in the form of ram, deer, shrew, eagle. Running. Wounded with arrows - the meat. Man tilts the heart. *Ut germen aptum próferens.* *Ut germen* - sprouts, seeds, invoked fruits, grains and clusters, exalted lava. *De um proterva* - nor the rock nor the ram can absolve his pain. Scars come back to him, they rule, they return - the flame from which he came. Without struggles, void of saying, falls. The man collapses in flesh linens. And the hours like a liturgy seal his scattering. He was killed by the discovered time: the open sky. Wooden Eve. Wax. Flame and breath - an idea of fire. The eve is a plain - a house. The eve is the house: only voice, breath. Clear rain falling -inert body. Sterile. Pure pain.

The Pendulum

Bring a pendulum

that scratches the darkness.

Treat the afternoon like a tigress

to let the light out

with its acrobatic tones.

Bring a spear

to stab the whole

flower.

Appearance of the devil.

The darkness came

with a message of water

open to light.

The eyes that go there

are of someone absurd

who insists on returning.

I Saw Death

I saw death on the benches

when that sad man came to the church.

Fleeting shrews were attached to

the cigarette: they sprouted from the light.

Maybe they were vague stars

painted in the vault. And they went down with him.

I saw the light. I saw the sun in strands,

that afternoon next to the man

on the temple's transept,

border of the sunset when the light trembles.

Naked he brought shadows and a blizzard. The

windstorm came very late. When he died.

Arches

Eternity spins

on a black stone;

lies buried,

captures the whisper of light

about to become night.

Flame and ogive

appear: a stony flower

of six petals, that gets more complex

in fleeting intermediate flowers

and two more petals come out.

Thus, it walks eternal in the stone

that nothing grown and present,

it gets dark the next day

with innumerable arches where

yesterday there were eight closed circles.

And the arches border a center

of long leaves to be

surrounded by vertical lights,

in an unravelling about to become a star.

The Last Level of Light

Will there be something beyond the last level of light?

The danger is the beast that dwells in the sunset,

the dazzled perfection.

So much light revives the monster:

that absurd pain

limping like a wounded deer,

the pack just in the blast of light;

a spire in the middle of the night

or an arch without columns. This

is how the beast appears

at the opposite pole of the shadow.

It is fear, motionless

as an instant, as a lost ray.

The battered clarity,

battered by the sun

- indifferent to the time that passes-

songs of prawn, the moments:

face to face they believe they are looking at the light.

Excess sunshine and the beast comes.

I want to tempt the bodies, their flesh,

to walk in the shade

there on the floor,

with the senses open to the dew

to know the light of noon

where

impregnable it lives, superluminous.

It dies wounded

-repose or silence-.

It will be opaque by being so fierce,

broken with its golden eye.

Paradise

That noise opens

and closes;

voices, vowels, a joyful heart.

A song.

The hinge opens

and closes, as if it vocalized

the paradise.

The jubilation of the untranslatable

song, dilates the voice,

extends in secret

the excess of light in the syllables:

ambiguity made soil.

I Am the Black Virgin

I am the virgin

look how opaque I am,

I have wheat in my hand,

the crops as a balance.

I am the black virgin,

dark by my chaos,

violent and warm;

I did not have the horoscope

in my hands,

I never knew how to see the sky,

nor did they give me the balance

that other women take

and put it on the breast

to be luminous.

I am the imperfect virgin,

the fields of unconscious ardor

impregnated me,

common swifts circled me

and I was in the middle of the field

three times pregnant,

alien to the earth.

I wanted to go after the angels,

to look for a place in the heavens,

I wanted lights, I wanted gusts.

I am the black virgin.

Without a future. Without dawn.

Go to the world to contemplate

other tones, I remain selfish

and silent,

I seek the light of the solstice,

the bravest and the most fearsome.

I want to see the shadow face to face.

I am -against the light-the opaque virgin.

Lute

... in a garden in a stone cathedral
(not built, no,
played in a lute) ...
WISLAWA SZYMBORSKA

Played in a lute

-out of stone the cathedral.

In a garden the lute vocalizes

the expansion of a psalm

-cathedral.

The lute plays where there is a garden,

there is no stone - nor construction –

it is the rope-glass: it vibrates in the stained glass,

the break of the "i" with a prayer.

Flute notes sketch ogives,

mourning the song with the stone.

From stone, the chimeras see

strings as longings, colors

on the shoulder blade.

Gorgons, girls,

opposite versions: venom and mercy:

gargoyles of the cathedral.

They spit on us. If there is sun on the stone

they are indifferent.

In the garden - on the sunset. At an acute angle. A
                                        [lute.

Chorus

Solar

The sun rose and now it was descending.

Instant where the solar

slope ends.

There lives a song, a prayer:

a turtle-lute.

It wants to escape to the high seas

but loves the stone.

It walks without a shell:

on its back it carries a lyre.

It shakes the darkness,

it does not let the sun go out, and it cries.

Face to face with the shadow

it suffocates the creatures:

it makes them the prey of acedia.

The inaccessible light

deprives the cosmos of heaven.

The Coven

The drop falls from the well to the ocean,

a flight of geese:

between my fingers the boundary,

drop by drop.

It's the confusion-because I loved him.

The tide goes up, the devils come,

they form a coven in my hands.

Sweat cracks them. It rains: twelve drops

fall on the jug. It's the time.

My numb hand is full

of ants: needles. The geese come

again-a thousand in my dreams.

Will he come back? Drops and shadow, shadows

and the mirror: there remains a vulture. Stalking.

In the canal the drops no longer irrigate peace.

Vulture and ocean are sting: victimizers.

I stay on the stone, waiting in the open.

Heartless but curious. I come back, I look for him.

I'm Lot. I prefer the stone.

Home

The house burns on four sides,

It's noon. An omen brings

the cry of the fire, the clarity

overturns.

Noon takes away the calm

of the intermediate hours.

Through that eye of the needle

of the time: peak: the news arrives

of the uselessness of life.

A mirror goes down and reveals

the calmness of the house, right there

where silence barely finds

shelter. It is the complete vision

of something incomprehensible. Translucent

insects:

are they the hours?

Incisors crush us to burn

in the total fire of the house.

Twelve O'Clock

Quarter to twelve.

The sill is filled with stones,

a lady covered with feathers

perverts the scene.

Ten to twelve.

A winged woman in search

of whoever discovers her falsehood,

she dances in the middle of the table,

wants to be sinister.

Five to Twelve.

Between woman and bird

it turns toward the air and the earth,

in the depths of itself.

Twelve o'clock.

An angel appears also false,

red and violent,

he believes he has a virgin in his hands.

Twelve o'clock.

The excess of light blazes the scene

to such an extent that the distance ends:

The landscape is gloomy:

threads of wings fall.

Twelve o'clock.

There is the woman,

facing the wall, behind bars.

In solitude.

Locked up and falsely crazy.

The Lady

Numb and with stiff body

the cataleptic lady orders

things of the world. To the bottom

of her hut, with nerves

jumping on the outside - hysterical lady –

wants a child with her uterus open.

Meanwhile, the particles

or the nonsense of the trees,

the hidden catapult,

or something from the cosmos that comes down

turns her into a witch: she guesses the future,

predicts the landslides, foresees

the crops, and even the disturbances of war.

The cataleptic lady, so still, crippled, moves

celestial spheres. She is not a saint, she has

-only-the uterus outside.

Catlike

Putting together a scheme goes the cat,

chalks and junks. The cat goes

oblique on the afternoon,

hidden in its enigma.

It separates the air and stupidly relates

-fleeting bow- the pleasures

of possessing claws, souring footprints,

undermining souls and pulling out a tree

and behind it a black-greenish sky.

It solidifies fury

to arrive at night

-orange blossoms and clovers- as if it were

any dog.

Fable

That no.

Not that either.

What for.

That yes.

That I go with you.

That when.

So argue the rooster and the mole,

one carved in the apse

looking at successful parishioners,

bored, suspicious,

escaping in any way to nonsense.

And it beat its wings.

The other one enraptured in the foundation,

collecting prayers, eating shadows,

and on its head a funeral spot:

bended bodies and blind memory.

The Hanged Man

The hanged man goes, dazzled

by that version of horizontal light

that jerks, sharpens and perverts.

Hanged like in the legend

he frightens those who see him,

turbulent his frenzy, his anguish,

though silent goes through the skin.

Free rein hangman, cordless,

no gimmicks. He walks alone and is sharp.

He is a shabby man who drank light

in a different way than you and me, a saw's

light, sharp, full of oblique beings,

punctilious, ridiculous but fierce

and truthful. He talks to the goats,

sleeps with bats,

hanging from the tree, hanged.

The Hump

The hump grows on Sundays,

foolishness or nectar, the tenderness

grows upside down, tremulous,

without voices, or perhaps many voices

all stuttering, indiscreet, as

stinging my own idea of life.

The hump becomes a great mountain

from which the landscape appears,

the skeletal nudity of things.

The hump is pure

filling, the roulette without a player. Chairs,

and luck also prowling alone.

It turns and nobody; it is the hump of the

commandments: by repeating and

enumerating the nothingness continue.

Perfect.

Crypt

Moon

As a plant that wakes up at night in plain full moon,
the girl drowned with light.

Snapshot

From the stained glass that forms the setting sun I look at myself. The trot of a horse whirls memories among dried leaves. My space, villages' snapshots of my body: a pillow, the edge of the bed, a shawl and my time separate me from the outside. If the surroundings are stone I'm alive, if I'm stone I have died and I soften.

Tombs

The Père Lachaise exists, its wheat tells you, the chestnuts scrawl in the sky, turning insurgents, looking to the east. To lean out and enter its oblique secret, in the latticed light. Open-mouthed the wind boils and a neon sign announces fashion. On the street sunset passes without looking at the mountain of tombs, the neon sign shines more, the cemetery gleams.

From the cafe, I see the night appear

and the stone angels die.

Shutters

In the extremity of the walls the dead

are breeding, in the old bodies

the crows are compressed

and vultures sense beauty.

There the noises of shutters

are staying, torn names

and the ups and downs of light on the tattooed skin.

Stone

The woman returned in stems,

in shadows and fragments of words,

from her coffin she is a compound mutilated

of things that are seen:

The ivy repeated without shape.

She would love to leave the land, giving things

a reflex to move, a soft hand

to remove the useless. Posing in the space.

The stone stops her.

Drop

Under the protection of, so as not to be

unraveled like a bird,

with my hands I formed vines,

I dressed up my face as a statue,

I sat under the trees

imploring a sky.

The nothingness happened.

The wall buffets

reproducing more walls,

agglomeration of spheres

every time smaller

until I am reduced to a drop.

Dream

They sent me to collect moons,

they all left.

The older siblings look for

other roads, leaving me with the house

among dark furniture.

I have been told to collect moons

in the window while they arrive.

But time forms itself into rings furiously,

strikes me against the night,

makes the doors creak,

lets the shadows pass, embedded

on my white dress.

Roots

The walls are cooled, cardboard slopes.

The leeches' nest grows

with its unbridled hunger, wanting to touch

the living from some vein, the last life,

penetrating the interior undermining it;

They rummage like cats and scratch

up to the rigidity of the nails. They can be satyrs

of unfeigned darkness and unfeigned light.

Wood gets wet, there are gaps in the patio

and countless roots: since I died I am fertile.

Tree

A child asks me how to leave the first

tree he saw: an anchor in his look, a perimeter

of impossible height. The child-tree mends the leaves,

ties down all the dead on the floor , comes into his

and waits.   [shell

Torso

A stain that is a black torso

comes back to me, the horse's cracks

look for me;

there are hands exhuming the earth

to find my trail.

Now seven thorns and a stem

form me. I escape the anguish,

escaping with the sap:

weightless trench that prevents me

from moving to the side.

Meridian

And then you do not return, you get to deal with
sand, sagacious hammers recognize you, time looks
for you like a prisoner and imprisoned it gallops over
you, ruminates its vexations, time does not adjust to
the meridian so you do not return.
And you lose your oval, the smile, you lose
the detail of your face and your own hideout.

Guardian Angel

The light was of salt;

waning moon your parted lips,

you passed over all my story

with the silent sensation of a suggested kiss.

In the rough waters the pulse of your body

touched my borders,

but how fine the texture of your mouth:

it was breath and touch,

barely brush and possession.

Christ

A terrace open to the night

was my mouth crossed in chords

by the bronze tones of your lips

they were incredulous steps first

later we found that bedroom

of the repeated breath

and the smell of apple trees exceeded

the limits of audacity.

The Kingdom of Autumn

In the gate the leaves fall apart

the clouds

are bright steel.

It is the turn of the old.

The tree is entangled in the fence

like a wrinkle on the cheekbone.

Towards Another Way

He enclosed my womb

growing moon

the illusion of a face

with eyes of sand

a body

with flashing blue veins

naked and almost blue

because of its whiteness

made of time

he approached growing

hair

lips

untenable

he sat waiting for me

I waited for him looking at the stars.

Banished from the air

with creases on his eyelids:

the forehead: a beach of light

Was it me?

waning moon

ash arms

on the deserted

now away from my blood

away from time

bird or angel

fish or embryo

clover or tree

he disappeared one sunrise

in the current towards a different way.

Drought

There is a moonless window
a herbless thread

bitter

geometric

sharp

the drought is in the mouth

and only behind the curtains
I hear them little by little kissing.

The Black Key

To die

      to press the black key

            matt crevice

where some trace awaits

to sink

      a tattoo on the back

by the tissues of the past

and to ferment

      the acute and white key

until you find the mouth of the earth

and return the gasps

to the night that will drink our yearnings.

Nocturnal

On marble those marine rollovers,

on opals the pulse of its fingers.

I knew about the statue

when a goodbye left it motionless,

with time

turned atoms.

I knew about the statue

in my own breath

cornered, empty of fluctuations.

I knew the horror of my skin

against its cold, impassable

texture.

Mob

To turn the corner

to sink the face

finding black feathers

flying ostriches that used to fly before

to turn the corner

to twist the back

and some wolves fleeing

when from other eyes

your gaze comes

and the tumult of voices

forms footsteps.

Index

PORTICO

The Angel   11

To a Virgin   12

Saint James   13

The Night   14

Devils   15

Land Devils   16

Igneous Devils   17

Colorless Devils   18

Air Devils   19

Silhouette   20

A window   21

Reflections   22

Mirage   23

The Land Thickens   24

Oratorium   25

Arch   26

STAIN GLASS

Sketch 29

Enduring Miracle 30

Black Virgin 31

Vault 32

St. Michael Archangel 34

Candles 35

The Monk 36

Shadows 38

Altar 40

Prayers 41

Tunic 42

Mask 43

Under the light 45

The Raven 46

The Last White Deer 47

Church 48

Olive Tree 49

Tapestry 50

Underground Lake   51

MAIN NAVE

The Space   55

There They Burn   56

The Oblique Lady   57

The Trap   58

Dazzled   59

Farnearness   61

Meanwhile   62

Channel   63

Wings   64

The Tall Cedar   65

Distance   66

SONGS

On the Eve   71

The Pendulum   72

I Saw Death   73

Arches 74

The Last Level of Light 75

Paradise 76

I Am the Black Virgen 77

Lute 78

CHORUS

Solar 85

The Coven 86

The House 87

Twelve O'clock 88

The Lady 90

Cat Like 91

Fable 92

The Hanged Man 93

The Hump 94

CRYPT

Moon 97

Snapshot 98

Tombs 99

Shutter 100

Stone 101

Drop 102

Dream 103

Roots 104

Tree 105

Torso 106

Meridian 107

Guardian Angel 108

Christ 109

The Kingdom of Autumn 110

Towards Another

Way 111

Drought 113

The Black Key 114

Nocturnal 115

Mob 116

About the Author

Silvia Eugenia Castillero was born in Mexico City. She is the author of the following books of essays: *Entre dos silencios, la poesía como experiencia* (Tierra Adentro, Mexico City, 1992 and 2003) and *Aberraciones: El ocio de las formas* (UNAM, 2008). In poetry, she has published *Como si despacio la noche* (Secretary of Culture of Jalisco, Guadalajara, 1993); *Nudos de luz*, with serigraphs by Rigoberto Padilla (Ediciones Sur and Universidad de Guadalajara, Guadalajara, 1995); *Zooliloquios*, (bilingual edition, French translation by Claude Couffon, Indigo Editions, Paris, 1997); *Zooliloquios, historia no natural* (CONACULTA, Colección Práctica Moral, Mexico City, 2003). *Eloísa*, (Editorial Aldus and Universidad de Guadalajara, Mexico City, 2010). *Héloïse* (Éditions du Noroît, French translation by Francois-Michel Durazzo, Montreal, 2012). *Eloise*, (Unicorn Press , Inc., English translation by Sarah Pollack, Greensboro, 2014).She was awarded the *Certamen Internacional Letras del Bicentenario Sor Juana Ines de la Cruz 2011* prize, in the poetry category with the book *En un laúd –la catedral* (Fondo Editorial EdoMex, 2012). She was also a finalist in the *III Certamen de Poesía Festival de la Lira 2011* contest for published work, in Cuenca, Ecuador, with her book *Eloísa*. She is currently director of the literary magazine *Luvina* of the University of Guadalajara. She is currently a Professor and Researcher in the Department of Letters at the CUCSH at the Univerity of Guadalajara, and member of the National System of Art Creators of Mexico, since 2007.

Author's photo by Mariano Aparicio

About the Translator

Victoria M. Contreras is a retired Professor of Linguistics and Pedagogy of Language. She taught in the Department of Modern Languages and Literatures at the University of Texas-Pan American, also serving as interim director thereof in 2000-2001. She graduated from the University of Texas at Austin where she received her doctorate in Foreign Language Education. Throughout her teaching career she has lectured in the United States and Spain. She is widely recognized in the field of applied linguistics, particularly for her research on Spanish for heritage speakers. As a translator she has collaborated with local and national institutions such as the Boys Club, International Airport of Mc Allen, the municipalities of Pharr, Edinburg and McAllen, University of Texas-Pan American, as well as law firms and hospitals. In the field of literary translation she edited the English translation of *El Corazón Transfigurado/ The Transfigured Heart* by Dolores Castro Varela (Libros Medio Siglo, 2013) and La Invencible/The Invincible by Vicente Quirarte. Dr. Contreras translated into English the following poetry books: *Callejón Kashaní / Kashani Alley* by Elvia Ardalani, *Nunca quise detener el tiempo / I Never Wanted to Stop Time* by Sara Uribe, *Reducido a polvo / Reduced to Dust* by Luis Vicente de Aguinaga, *Cacerías /Hunting* by Oliverio Arreola and *Theory of Losses* by Jesús Ramón Ibarra among others.

Poetry Books in Libros Medio Siglo

Eyes Already Ruined – Luis Aguilar

Reduced to Dust – Luis Vicente de Aguinaga

The Being of the Household Beings – Elvia Ardalani

The Drunkenness of God – Luis Armenta Malpica

Hunting – Oliverio Arreola

In a Lute – The Cathedral – Silvia Eugenia Castillero

The Transfigured Heart – Dolores Castro Varela

Something Pains the Wind – Dolores Castro Varela

Theory of Losses – Jesús Ramón Ibarra

The Invincible – Vicente Quirarte

Nave Sorda – René Rodríguez Soriano

I Never Wanted to Stop Time – Sara Uribe